NEW YORK
THEN & NOW

NEW YORK
THEN & NOW

ANNETTE WITHERIDGE

Thunder Bay
P·R·E·S·S

Thunder Bay Press
An imprint of the Advantage Publishers Group
5880 Oberlin Drive, San Diego, CA 92121-4794
www.advantagebooksonline.com

Produced by PRC Publishing Ltd,
8–10 Blenheim Court, Brewery Road, London, N7 9NY, England.

A member of the Chrysalis Group plc

ISBN 1-57145-797-6

Library of Congress Cataloging-in-Publication Data available upon request.

Picture credits:
The black and white photographs are credited at the end of each caption. Our thanks to the staff of the
New York Historical Society photographic department for their assistance with the research for this project.
All color photographs are by Simon Clay unless individually credited.

Acknowledgments:
Thanks to Simon and Sandra Forty, Susan Philip, and Louise Daubeny for photo research.

Cover and Back Cover: The difference 62 years make — the Port of New York from the air in 1933 and 1995. © *The Mariners'
Museum/Corbis;* © *Gail Mooney/Corbis*

Page 1 and Page 2: The Hopkins Store (see pages 32–33).

Above: Arrival of the Alexandrian Obelisk — Cleopatra's Needle — at the foot of 96th Street in 1879.
© *Collection of the New-York Historical Society, negative number 69481*

INTRODUCTION

New York is fondly known as the capital city of the world, yet until the 17th century the only inhabitants were Native Americans. The Indians and the Dutch began trading in 1610. In 1621 a group of merchants organized the West India Company and the first Dutch settlers arrived in Manhattan in 1623. In 1626 Peter Minuit bought the island from the Manhattan Indians for a handful of trinkets worth $24.

By the 1660s the settlement had 270 residents and its first municipal government. The English snatched Manhattan in 1664 after Charles II gave the colony to his brother the Duke of York. For the next century New York muddled along, but high taxes united the settlers in their dislike of the British.

During the American Revolution, the British hung onto Manhattan for seven years until 1783, when America claimed victory over England in the War of Independence. For the next six years New York was the capital of America but after his election as president, George Washington moved the government to Philadelphia and then Washington, D.C.

Ignoring its loss of federal supremacy, New York expanded rapidly and by the 1800s the population had tripled to 100,000. By 1811 city commissioners had laid out Manhattan streets as a checkerboard of 2,026 rectangular blocks. Ironically, most of the city was still swamp land and pitifully unprepared for around three million European immigrants who arrived seeking the American dream.

While commerce thrived, the poor lived in appalling slums. As work began to relieve the overcrowding, the Civil War broke out in 1861 and ambitious building plans were put on hold. But after the war Manhattan expanded in spectacular style. The Brooklyn Bridge, the New York Public Library, and the Metropolitan Museum were completed; grand mansions sprang up along Fifth Avenue; and department stores were built to cater to the needs of New York's rich.

The race for the sky began in 1902 with the Fuller Building — quickly nicknamed the Flatiron because of its triangular shape — and Frank Woolworth's 792-foot tower followed to become the world's tallest structure in 1913.

In 1930 the Chrysler became the tallest building, only to lose the title to the Empire State Building one year later. The 1,454-foot structure retained its "world's tallest" tag until 1973 when the World Trade Center's twin towers were built.

Financier John Rockefeller's dream city-within-a-city began to take shape in the Depression and the complex covering 11 acres includes 19 buildings, Radio City Music Hall, a 5,900-seat theatre, and the studios of the National Broadcasting Company (NBC), along with shops and restaurants.

Glass boxes, steel structures, and stone monstrosities followed as New York expanded upward. But Manhattan's nonchalant attitude to knocking down the old and bringing in the new horrified conservationists, and when the once spectacular Pennsylvania Station was demolished in 1965, the New York Landmark Trust was created to preserve the city's old buildings.

Today New York is a dramatic blend of old and new and its skyline is instantly recognizable around the world. In this book we hope to capture the very best — and sometimes the worst — of New York and its changing vista.

Annette Witheridge
New York, 1999

She is known the world over as the symbol of America and provided the first glimpse of New York for millions of immigrants arriving by boat. The Statue of Liberty was a gift from France. Designed by Frédéric Auguste Bartholdi, the 225-ton statue is based on a likeness of his mother. This is an 1890 Artotype by Bierstadt. © *Collection of the New-York Historical Society, negative number 50593*

Embarrassingly, lack of funds to build the statue's pedestal was a problem, and it took nine years to raise enough money for the base (see page 68). It was finally unveiled in 1886 and the 151-foot tall statue remains one of New York's main tourist attractions. It is still possible to climb up the spiral staircase into the crown. © *Gail Mooney/Corbis*

Named after the battery of cannon protecting the tip of Manhattan, Battery Park provided immigrants with their first taste of New York. Built in 1807 to protect Manhattan from British forces, Castle Clinton has gone through several changes of use, having been a theater, an immigration center, and an aquarium. This 1883 view of Battery Park includes Trinity Church steeple. © *Collection of the New-York Historical Society, negative number 2528*

Today Castle Clinton (inset), minus its roof, serves as the ticket office for the Statue of Liberty–Ellis Island ferry, and is the main visitors' center for National Park Service sites in Manhattan. To the right of Castle Clinton, visible above the trees, is Number One Broadway. Originally built as the Washington Building in 1884, it was redesigned with a new renaissance front in 1922. It originally housed several steamship companies and the façades are decorated with seashells, dolphins, and the shields of port cities.

When the immigrants caught their first glimpse of New York on January 21, 1934, the Manhattan skyline was already impressive. Companies were outdoing each other to build the tallest and grandest buildings. © *Collection of the New-York Historical Society, negative number 73105*

This desire to create the tallest and grandest buildings culminated in the early 1970s with the World Trade Center, begun in 1966. The WTC complex encompassed not only the twin towers but seven skyscraping office buildings and a massive underground shopping concourse. Architects Minoru Yamasaki and Emory Roth designed the towers using tubular engineering to reach the stunning heights of 1,368 and 1,362 feet for towers one and two, respectively.

The buildings of the historical financial district are dwarfed by looming sky-scrapers, but the sheer size of the World Trade Center at left outdoes them all. Before 1974, the twin towers were the tallest buildings in the world, symbolizing the soaring pride of New York City. On February 26, 1993, the WTC was the target of a terrorist bombing that killed six people and injured thousands. The towers withstood the blast, however, and reopened within a month.

On the morning of September 11, 2001, in a despicable act of terrorism, the World Trade Center's twin towers sustained direct hits by two hijacked commercial jetliners. Although designed to withstand impact, the towers could not survive the resulting fires. Shortly after the attack, both towers collapsed, killing thousands. This photograph taken over a week later shows the still smoldering ruins in the midst of the world's most recognizable skyline.

Wall Street became the focal point of New York life in 1653 when early settlers built a wall across lower Manhattan to protect themselves from the British in New England. By 1870, when this photograph was taken, the area was the hub of Manhattan's commerce with the Subtreasury Building and the rebuilt Trinity Church looming over shops and offices. © *Collection of the New-York Historical Society, negative number 50741*

The original Trinity Church (1698) was burned during the Revolutionary War. It was followed by another in the late 1700s, which was demolished fifty years later. At 281 feet, the third and final Trinity Church, built in 1846, was the tallest building in New York for 42 years and was visible 15 miles out to sea. By the end of the 19th century it was dwarfed by surrounding skyscrapers, but even today its brownstone spire still provides an impressive view down Wall Street.

America was in the midst of the Great Depression when this photograph of Broad Street and the corner of Wall Street was taken in the 1930s. Even though the surrounding New York streets were full of shanty structures and soup kitchens, the financial district maintained an aura of wealth. *Hulton Getty Picture Collection*

Building work and renovations continue along Wall and Broad streets, home
to the ornate New York Stock Exchange and financial institutions like
J. P. Morgan and Company and the Bankers Trust. The Corinthian-columned
Exchange was completed in 1903, but today it jostles for attention along
crowded Broad Street.

The streetcar era was at its height when this photograph was taken along Broadway in 1888. Streetcars rumbled along every few minutes and stopped outside the original Western Union Building, with its distinctive clock tower. Canopies, allowing shopkeepers to display their wares outside, protruded from many of the buildings.
© *Collection of the New-York Historical Society, negative number 33551*

The American Telephone & Telegraph headquarters building erected in 1917 at 195 Broadway. The Renaissance Revival building was designed by Welles Bosworth and the lobby is a forest of Doric columns.

A bustling Broadway, as seen from Barclay Street, shows a tangle of electric lines and horse-drawn carts jostling for space alongside the streetcars that were increasingly the fastest way of getting around New York. Note the canopies on the ground-floor business fronts — in the summer they gave protection from the heat and in the winter from rain. © *Collection of the New-York Historical Society, negative number 33624*

The tangle of electric wires and streetcar tracks have gone, replaced by street lamps and cars. The old five- and six-story townhouse buildings were demolished and replaced by towering skyscrapers. The small independent merchants of yesteryear disappeared when the big business corporations moved in.

Trinity Church,

Church spires were once the focal point of New York, dotting the Manhattan skyline. They provided handy meeting places and Trinity Church, sitting near the busy junction with Exchange Alley, was no exception. Shoppers and workers alike congregated near the entrance as businesses pulled down the shutters every evening. This photograph, dated around 1887, looks north up the west side of Broadway. © *Collection of the New-York Historical Society, negative number 57026*

The church remains but the view along Broadway at Exchange Alley is very different today. A giant skyscraper now overshadows the Gothic spire and the small businesses are gone, replaced by modern office blocks. The building explosion along this part of Broadway began in the 1920s and the Art Deco structures were dubbed "Modern Classics."

Far left: New Yorkers were intrigued by the fast rising Singer Building as it was being built in 1907. The 612-foot tall structure was the city's tallest building and among the modern conveniences inside was a special vacuum machine for polishing top hats. In the future, 149 Broadway would become notorious for the amount of suicides it attracted. © *Collection of the New-York Historical Society, negative number 64200-493D*

Left: Manhattan's skyline changed year by year and this aerial shot of the Singer Building dated July 1, 1912, shows the ornate tower overshadowing surrounding buildings including the 12-story "Little" Singer Building, an avant-garde terra cotta, wrought iron, and glass structure built in 1904, a few blocks further up Broadway. *Hulton Getty Picture Collection*

Right: When the Singer Building was demolished in 1967 it earned another dubious title — this time for the tallest structure ever to be torn down. Again New Yorkers crowded to watch as the wreckers went in and another modern block quickly went up in its place. Surprisingly, some of the old nearby buildings have survived the century.

Back in 1890, Broadway at its junction with Fulton and Vesey streets was a busy intersection and streetcar terminal. A multitude of small businesses, from greengrocers and pharmacies to up-market luggage stores and gentlemen's outfitters, vied for passing trade. The building was the Astor House, one of the cities leading hotels, built in 1836. It was demolished in two stages in 1916 and 1926. The photograph also shows, at left, St. Paul's Chapel, built in 1766, attributed to Thomas McBean.
© *Collection of the New-York Historical Society, negative number 43486*

The building in this location today was built in 1927 as the Astor Building; now it is known as 217 Broadway and is home to a dozen stores and offices. Originally designed to look over the Hudson, the Broadway entrance is now used as the main entrance. The streetcars have been replaced by buses, cars, and the inevitable yellow cabs. Some of lower Manhattan's most impressive skyscrapers can be seen in the background, including the former World Trade Center. St. Paul's Chapel is still there, today, the oldest surviving church in Manhattan.

Left: This photograph of the newly completed Woolworth Building is taken from the northeast and shows the roof of City Hall and the old Post Office building. The Woolworth Building was built and paid for in cash by chain store magnate Frank Woolworth. The 761-foot building, complete with gargoyles, was finished in 1913 and the 60-story skyscraper remained the tallest building in the world until the Chrysler was completed in 1930. The marble lobby boasts a glass and mosaic ceiling. © *Collection of the New-York Historical Society, negative number 46809*

Right: Woolworth closed its New York stores in 1997, but founder Frank Woolworth's skyscraper remains as impressive as ever, nestling between the towers of the former World Trade Center. Intrepid visitors have been known to take the elevators to the 54th floor and then climb a spiral staircase to an observation deck surrounded by gargoyles of frogs, pelicans and bats.

New York's City Hall, completed in 1812, remains one of America's most beautiful buildings. Joseph-François Mangin and John McComb's design was the winning entry of an 1802 contest to create the ultimate local government office. Inside, the main entrance hall leads to a spectacular rotunda with a pair of cantilevered stairs curving upward. This view from the south was taken in 1892. © Collection of the New-York Historical Society, negative number 1731

City Hall with its tree-lined square park remains as dramatic today as it did in the early 1800s, but over the years the exterior stonework of Massachusetts marble and brownstone deteriorated badly. It was replaced by a mixture of Alabama limestone and Missouri granite in 1956, and restoration work continues to this day.

Left: This photograph was taken in 1893 from the *New York Tribune* newspaper office across Broadway to the block between Park Place and Murray Street. On the right edge of the photograph is the dramatic Hopkins Store, an 1857 Venetian Renaissance-inspired building built by glasswork manufacturers Francis and John Hopkins. The park was a popular promenade for courting couples. Just out of the photograph at right is City Hall. © *Collection of the New-York Historical Society, negative number 52555*

Right: The Hopkins Store, converted into an exclusive apartment building in 1996, is just visible in the center dwarfed by the surrounding skyscrapers — including at far left the Woolworth Building in front of the former World Trade Center. The glint of water in the background is a reminder that Manhattan is an island dotted between the fast-flowing Hudson and East rivers and the sea.

Broadway at Fulton Street and Park Place was a busy intersection in 1866, and pedestrians, fed up with vying for road space with horse-drawn carriages, marveled at the new Loew footbridge. It became a popular meeting place for courting couples who, dressed in their Sunday best, would view the goings-on below. © *Collection of the New-York Historical Society, negative number 56029*

After the footbridge was demolished there was a far better view of St. Paul's
Chapel and the dramatic skyscrapers that now dominate Broadway's skyline.
Note how the road has also been widened to accommodate the traffic. But on
weekends, when businesses are closed, it is still a popular spot for sightseeing.

Left: The intersection of Broadway and Grand Street in 1860, as seen in this photograph by Roege, was almost as congested with traffic then as it is today. The only difference was the mode of traffic, with horse-drawn carriages being the favorite. This area of Broadway was just beginning to become popular with art lovers, as galleries sprang up among the shops.

© Collection of the New-York Historical Society, negative number 9229

Right: Today Broadway is home to hundreds of artists, who moved into the spacious but untrendy loft apartments in the 1960s and 1970s. Nowadays the rents are sky high but the artists are ploughing their talents back into the area.

The busy fruit and vegetable market at the junction of Hester and Norfolk streets is seen in 1898. The area was home to thousands of Jewish and Italian families who lived in appallingly crowded conditions after leaving their homelands in the 1880s for a new life and dreams of riches beyond their wildest imaginations. © *Collection of the New-York Historical Society, negative number 37363*

Lower Manhattan is still considered to be a working class area, although the junction of Hester and Norfolk streets has been gentrified. Trees now line the streets and tall apartment buildings have replaced the scruffy low buildings of yesteryear. Nowadays the intersection resembles dozens of other city streets and the market has been replaced by greengrocers and delis.

Fulton Street was arguably the busiest street in New York when the fish market opened in 1821. This photograph of the Fulton Ferry offices at the foot of Fulton Street and Burling Slip, on South Street, was taken in about 1876. The steam-powered ferry service between Manhattan and Brooklyn began in 1814 and led to a surge of other building in the area. Gothic structures and dramatic Greek revival office blocks sprung up in the surrounding streets. © *Collection of the New-York Historical Society, negative number 47587*

Historians blame the opening of the Brooklyn Bridge in 1883 for killing trade around
Fulton Street. But the area is enjoying a revival as the South Street Seaport — a complex
that covers seven blocks and extends over three piers, including Pier 17 as illustrated — is
once again bustling with shops and restaurants. The old ferry house was demolished many
years ago.

New Yorkers joke that the fishy smell surrounding South Street can cure a cold in twenty minutes: in the 1890s, when this photograph of sailing ships docked at the Old Slip was taken, the smell must have been unbearable. Aside from the deliveries of fish, South Street was a hub for craft filled with exotic cargoes from around the world. The Brooklyn Bridge can just be made out through the masts and rigging. © *Collection of the New-York Historical Society, negative number 44117*

Today South Street Seaport is an odd mixture of restaurants, trendy shops, street musicians, tennis courts, and old ships. Often described by disparaging New Yorkers as a maritime theme park, it provides a much-needed cool breeze from the water in the height of summer and is often host to visiting historic ships. Here are two fixtures: alongside Pier 16 the *Peking* built in Germany in 1911, and at Pier 15 the *Wavertree* built in England in 1885.

Above: Brooklyn Bridge, which took sixteen years and 600 men to build, is often described as the greatest engineering work of the Victorian age. This fabulous view of the New York skyline was taken by J. H. Beals from the East River's far from complete bridge in 1876, and catches the mighty Hudson River in the distance. © *Collection of the New-York Historical Society, negative numbers 32183-32185*

Left: What a difference a century makes. In this photograph taken from the Brooklyn Bridge, the Hudson River was completely blocked out by the former World Trade Center and the huge financial district buildings that make the lower tip of Manhattan one of the most recognizable skylines in the world.

Right: Detail of the South Street Seaport Museum, showing the *Peking*.

Brooklyn Bridge was the brainchild of German immigrant John Augustus Roebling, who claimed that even if all the suspension cables snapped at once the bridge would merely sag. He died a week before the bridge got planning permission but his son, Colonel Washington Roebling, finally completed his work in 1883. This photograph is dated January 1, 1884. *Hulton Getty Picture Collection*

Brooklyn residents campaigned for the first bridge across the East River immediately after the Civil War. Roebling's original plans were thought to be a folly; however, the spectacular suspension bridge today offers some of the finest views of Manhattan.

When Brooklyn Bridge finally opened in 1883, its walkway was quickly filled by curious pedestrians. Many feared for their lives as the bridge creaked and swayed in the wind, so the following year circus owner P. T. Barnum led twenty-four elephants across from Manhattan to Brooklyn to prove it was safe. *Hulton Getty Picture Collection*

Despite the noise and pollution from the bridge's roadway twelve feet below,
the pedestrian walkway is still considered to be one of New York's most
romantic spots and is a popular place to watch the city's dramatic red sunsets.
At lunchtimes it resembles a running track with office workers jogging across.

These five-story brick buildings with wrought-iron balconies were popular in Tribeca at the end of the 19th century. By 1915, when this photograph was taken, huge commercial warehouses were dotted between the apartment buildings. Duane and Varick streets were considered to be the heart of the bustling trading center. © *Collection of the New-York Historical Society, negative number 368*

By the 1960s the major businesses had moved out of traffic-clogged Tribeca and the area became a deserted backwater. But artists began to move in during the 1970s and, since then, warehouse conversions have sent rents rocketing and turned Duane and Varick streets into one of the most sought-after residential districts of Manhattan. The buildings to the left no longer exist, but this similar building on modern day Duane Street gives a good impression of the changes that have taken place in the area.

Bleecker Street, in the heart of Greenwich Village, was a busy mix of commercial properties and apartments when this photograph was taken in 1896. The dark winter morning makes the street at the intersection with Thompson and Sullivan streets look grim, but on a warm day the area would be bustling with traders and shoppers. © *Collection of the New-York Historical Society, negative number 4633*

A century on and the five-story brick building has been sandblasted and the second-floor canopy is gone, but the facade has hardly changed. Trendy shops now occupy the ground floor, while upstairs are some of the most sought-after apartments in Greenwich Village.

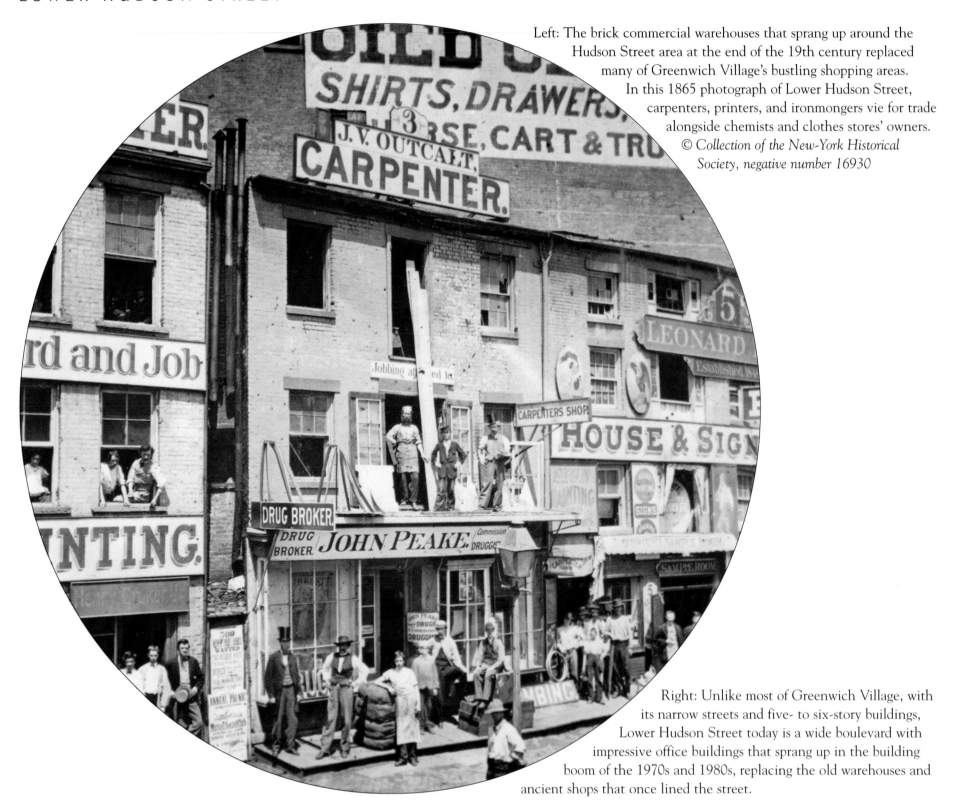

Left: The brick commercial warehouses that sprang up around the Hudson Street area at the end of the 19th century replaced many of Greenwich Village's bustling shopping areas. In this 1865 photograph of Lower Hudson Street, carpenters, printers, and ironmongers vie for trade alongside chemists and clothes stores' owners.
© Collection of the New-York Historical Society, negative number 16930

Right: Unlike most of Greenwich Village, with its narrow streets and five- to six-story buildings, Lower Hudson Street today is a wide boulevard with impressive office buildings that sprang up in the building boom of the 1970s and 1980s, replacing the old warehouses and ancient shops that once lined the street.

In 1889 a wooden arch was hastily erected in Washington Square at Fifth Avenue to commemorate the centennial of President George Washington's inauguation. The arch, complete with an 11-foot high wooden statue of America's first statesman, was designed by Stanford White and paid for by private subscription. © *Collection of the New-York Historical Society, negative number 49469*

Stanford White replaced his wooden arch with this magnificent 77-foot stone structure in 1892, now known as the gateway to Greenwich Village. After Fred Astaire was featured dancing on top of it in *The Belle of New York*, it holds the dubious distinction of being one of the most popular meeting places for blind dates. At the time of this photograph one of the twin towers of the former World Trade Center could be seen in the distance.

Jefferson Market Courthouse, pictured here in 1901, was voted America's fifth favorite building in the 1880s. Drawing from the ornate designs of medieval castles, the Victorian Gothic structure was designed by Calvert Vaux, one of Central Park's most spirited designers, and Frederick Clarke Withers. It originally served as a fire watch tower. © *Collection of the New-York Historical Society, negative number 65447*

Trees now block the view today, but the turreted tower of Jefferson Market Courthouse still looms up on the corner of Sixth Avenue and 10th Street. Originally standing upright in the midst of the city jail and court complex, the red and white-striped structure was restored in 1967 and is now used as a library.

This section of Fifth Avenue was once home to New York's wealthiest and most fashionable residents. Great mansions, like the ones shown here in 1892 at the junction with 16th Street, lined the wide boulevard, and horse-drawn carriages were the preferred mode of transport for women who did not want their skirts muddied on the surrounding unpaved streets. © *Collection of the New-York Historical Society, negative number 1030*

As fortunes tumbled during the Great Depression so did the great houses of Fifth Avenue. In their place sprang up commercial buildings. Today the section around 16th Street is literally home to the beautiful people. Model agencies have moved in, bringing trendy boutiques and chic coffee shops with them.

Union Square nestles between 14th and 17th streets, and the bronze statue of Washington marks the spot were the victorious general was greeted by New York's grateful citizens in 1783 after the British fled Manhattan. The statue was designed by Henry Kirke Brown in 1856. Soapbox orators, political agitators, and illegal demonstrators converged on Union Square almost weekly during the first half of the century. Nowadays, with spectacular views of the Empire State Building to the north, it is a gentrified park. The early photograph is dated about 1870. © *Collection of the New-York Historical Society, negative number 1995*

Originally called the Fuller Building, this 286-foot
21-story building was nicknamed the Flatiron because of
its dramatic wedge shape. Built in 1902 by Daniel H.
Burnham and Co., it signified the start of New York's
skyscraper-building era. Pictured here in 1910, there are
no surrounding buildings to rival its prominent position.
Hulton Getty Picture Collection

It is still possible to snatch the odd dramatic view of the Flatiron but nowadays the Renaissance Revival building is dwarfed by a multitude of larger structures. However, from Fifth Avenue the eagle-eyed passer-by can see the ornate limestone decorations, including the carved faces.

Madison Square began life as a burial ground for yellow fever victims and became a military drilling ground before it was turned into a park in 1847. This 1895 photograph shows the glamorous apartment buildings that lined the square. In later years, the statue-filled park lost its sophisticated image to the nearby Flatiron Building. *Hulton Getty Picture Collection*

This view looking up Broadway at 25th Street, to the left of the Worth Monument, shows the modern Madison Square, now overshadowed by the dramatic skyscrapers belonging to the Metropolitan Life and New York Life Insurance Companies. The once tranquil garden is now a bustling meeting place for joggers, lunchtime snackers, and young mothers.

Left: This photograph shows the Statue of Liberty's arm and torch plonked down on the edge of Madison Square Park as part of New York's embarrassing campaign to raise funds for the statue's plinth. The city fathers figured the wealthy residents passing through the park would be shamed into contributing. It took a while to work: it was not until spring 1884 that the first stone of the plinth, designed by Richard Morris Hunt, was laid.

This photograph looks north from 23rd Street up Fifth Avenue and Broadway. © *Collection of the New-York Historical Society, negative number 49251*

Right: The Statue of Liberty has long been reunited with her arm and now stands proudly as the gateway into New York Harbor. Her tranquil surroundings contrast with the now noisy Madison Square, which sits at the traffic and pedestrian-clogged intersection of Fifth Avenue, Broadway, and 23rd Street.

Madison Square's surrounding streets became the home of the rich and fashionable in the 1880s. Grand hotels like Delmonico's and the Fifth Avenue Hotel were quickly built to complement the brownstone mansions. This 1855 photograph shows well-dressed residents strolling along the newly paved sidewalk on Fifth Avenue. © *Collection of the New-York Historical Society, negative number 9248*

As the Great Depression struck New York in the 1930s, the fortunes of Manhattan's wealthy disappeared overnight and the grand mansions were shuttered or sold off as cheap apartment buildings. Today Fifth Avenue's fortunes are back on the upswing but few can afford to live in these sought-after properties.

This remarkable piece of work is the temporary triumphal arch and associated decorations erected on Fifth Avenue to welcome home soldiers returning from Europe after the First World War, a conflict that the United States had entered in 1917. Seen from 23rd Street looking north, despite its air of permanence, the arch was made of timber and was pulled down shortly afterward. © *Collection of the New-York Historical Society, negative number 1047*

Today nothing is left of the triumphal arch. What is clearly visible, however, is the Worth Monument, a 51-foot high obelisk that marks the remains and commemorates the bravery of Major General Williams Jenkins Worth who fought in the Mexican War of 1846–48. Designed by James Goodwin Batterson, it was erected in 1857.

Macy's was started by Rowland Hussey Macy, a one-time whaler, in 1857. He left his mark on the business in more ways than one: the red star trademark is said to be a representation of one tattooed on his arm! In 1902 the store outgrew its original location and moved to Herald Square. This photograph is dated 1905. *Hulton Getty Picture Collection*

Today, only the advertising billboards make a substantial difference. Since its move from 14th Street in 1902, Macy's has become world famous and, despite the ups and downs of the century, continues to live up to its self-proclaimed slogan — "The World's Largest Store." © *Lynn Goldsmith/Corbis*

William Waldorf Astor demolished his mansion in 1893 to spite his overbearing aunt, who lived next door, and built this spectacular hotel — the Hotel Waldorf. She responded by building the Astoria next door and promptly moved uptown, along with the rest of New York's elite. The two hotels were later joined by connecting corridors.
© *Collection of the New-York Historical Society, negative number 16576*

The Waldorf-Astoria Hotel moved to midtown in 1929 and over the next year and 45 days New Yorkers watched in amazement as the 1,250-foot Empire State Building shot up in its place. Probably now the most recognizable structure in America, it originally struggled to find tenants and was dubbed the "Empty" State Building.

Pennsylvania Station, along with its "sister" building the U.S. General Post Office across the street, was the crowning glory in the careers of fabled architects McKim, Mead, and White. The many-columned building, completed in 1913 and home to the Pennsylvania Railroad, was based on the Roman Baths of Caracalla. This photograph by Roege is from 1923. © *Collection of the New-York Historical Society, negative number 59171*

This glass monstrosity proved to be the catalyst for New York to establish the Landmarks Preservation Society. History buffs were rightly horrified when Penn Station was torn down in 1963 and have since fought tooth and nail to preserve the city's remaining archietctural masterpieces, including the once-doomed Grand Central.

Left: The tragic loss of Penn Station is shown off to perfection in these photographs. Flamboyant architect Stanford White, murdered on the roof of one of his own buildings by the deranged husband of his chorus girl mistress, and colleagues Charles Follen McKim and William Rutherford Mead let their imaginations run wild inside Penn Station. The domed ceilings and Roman columns dwarf the travelers seen in the main waiting room and ticket office in 1911 in a photograph taken by George P. Hall and Sons.
© *Collection of the New-York Historical Society, negative number 59167*

Right: Rarely a moment goes by when a New Yorker isn't complaining about the loss of old Penn Station and the ugliness of its replacement. Described as a jukebox oil-drum when it was built in 1966, the busy station looks shabby and dated, with its cheap souvenir shops, scruffy cafes, squashed together ticket kiosks and a bland waiting area.

Daylight floods through the gigantic windows of Grand Central Terminal in this classic photograph by George P. Hall and Sons. Railroad magnate Cornelius Vanderbilt's crowning glory was completed in 1913 and included a nine-story catwalk so that the adventurous could scale the windows. In its heyday, a red carpet was rolled out nightly for passengers boarding the train to Chicago. *© Collection of the New-York Historical Society, negative number 70587*

Four years of painstaking renovations at Grand Central were completed in 1998, once again exposing the incredible vaulted ceiling showing the night sky painted backward! The artists said it would allow travelers to picture the stars as God would have seen them. Jacqueline Kennedy Onassis headed the restoration campaign.

The first Grand Central Rail Depot in 1880 was home to the New York, Harlem and New-Haven Railroad. With its stage coach terminus in front, the new rail depot turned midtown into prime real estate. Today's Park Avenue, the previously scruffy shanty street called Fourth Avenue, became a desirable residential area. This photograph is dated 1886. © *Collection of the New-York Historical Society, negative number 2669*

Grand Central's beaux arts building is still dominated by a 13-foot clock and Jules Coutan's sculpture of Mercury, the God of Commerce, Minerva, Hercules, and the American symbol of an eagle. Elevated roadways now span both sides of the terminal and tall buildings jostle for space alongside architects' Warren and Wetmore's masterpiece.

The Chrsyler Building became the tallest building in the world when it was completed in 1930, topping France's 1880 engineering feat the Eiffel Tower and dominating the skyline around 42nd Street. The 1,046-foot Art Deco skyscraper, decorated with stainless steel gargoyles representing the auto industry, lost its world title to the Empire State Building a year later.
Hulton Getty Picture Collection

The Chrysler is often described as New York's Christmas tree and it can be seen twinkling in the darkness for miles around. Ironically, the metal spire was pushed through the roof and bolted down in just 90 minutes after architect William Van Alen discovered his rivals at 40 Wall Street were likely to top his tall building.

Left: The United Nations was formed in 1945 at the end of the most devastating war in history — the Second World War. In a world dominated by superpowers, it was fitting that New York City rather than a European capital was chosen as the location for the U.N. headquarters. The land on which the complex was built was purchased with the help of a donation by John D. Rockefeller, and deemed an international zone, not part of the United States. This photograph, taken on November 19, 1949, shows the Secretariat Building under construction. *Hulton Getty Picture Collection*

Right: Today the 17–18-acre U.N. site is the hub of world politics. The U.N. Security Council and the General Assembly both meet here with the aim of preserving world peace. The statue by Evgeny Vuchetich — "Let Us Beat Swords Into Plowshares" — in the U.N.'s riverside garden sums up this noble cause. © *Michael S. Yamashita/Corbis*

The Great Depression, which ended many ambitious building plans, had just begun when this rooftop picture was taken by Irving Browning in 1930. The Chrysler was New York's crowning glory but the *Daily News* Building to its left, along with the Chanin, Lincoln, and Lecourt Colonial buildings, also dominated 42nd Street's skyline. © *Collection of the New-York Historical Society, negative number 57909*

Taken from the 33-floor Churchill apartment building on Second Avenue, the Chrysler's spire can still be seen but the *Daily News* Building and other 1920s skyscrapers have been obscured by midtown's luxury residential blocks that began springing up in the 1960s and 1970s. The red and white brick Hightower now dominates.

The automobile, Henry Ford and Walter Chrysler's contribution to the American dream, was really starting to dominate New York when this photograph was taken at the busy intersection of Fifth Avenue and 42nd Street in 1925. Tall buildings springing up along the street are beginning to block out the sunlight. *Hulton Getty Picture Collection*

The intersection of Fifth Avenue and 42nd Street is still busy. Many of the older buildings have been demolished since 1925, and Fifth Avenue now gives off an aura of space. The junction is now a favorite of shoppers and tourists heading to nearby Bryant Park. The main photograph looks up Fifth Avenue from the southeast corner of the intersection. Inset is the view from the Public Library with St. Patrick's just visible on the left.

Health and sanitary conditions greatly improved from 1842 when water from Croton Lake was transported forty miles via underground pipes and an aqueduct to the Croton Reservoir, on the corner of Fifth Avenue and 42nd Street. But the system had become outdated by the time this photograph was taken by Robert Bracklow in 1899. © *Collection of the New-York Historical Society, negative number 60898*

The Croton Reservoir was demolished in 1899 to make way for New York's Public Library. Thomas M. Carrere and Thomas Hastings' beaux arts 1911 masterpiece was opened by President William Howard Taft. Scupltor E. C. Potter's lions, Patience and Fortitude, guard an incredible 92 miles of books stored underneath adjoining Bryant Park.

The 35-story McGraw-Hill Building on the Avenue of the Americas and 42nd Street is considered to be skyscraper architect Raymond Hood's greatest work. Completed in 1931, it became the role model for later structures with its blue-green terracotta facing and apple-green colored windows. The company's name was spelled out on top in 11-foot tall letters. Photograph by Samuel H. Gottscho. © *Collection of the New-York Historical Society, negative number 73107*

Publisher McGraw-Hill moved its printing presses out of its landmark building in the 1960s and nowadays the once-glorious structure, sitting on West 42nd Street at the junction with Sixth Avenue, is owned by an insurance company. But the eagle-eyed passer-by can still see sparkling colors from street level.

Longacre Square was renamed Times Square in 1904, the year this photograph was taken, in honor of the *New York Times* Building. The home to the city's most respected newspaper was completed that year, and New Year's Eve revelers switched from their old gathering place at Trinity Church to celebrate New Year's Eve in the square for the first time. © *Collection of the New-York Historical Society, negative number 67730*

Now often referred to as the "Old Gray Lady," the *New York Times* and the building named after it are barely noticeable amidst the garish neon lights and gawdy buildings that now occupy Times Square, Broadway and 42nd Street. The newspaper built a French chateau style complex nearby when it outgrew the tower block in 1913. (It may be seen in the photograph on page 101.)

By 1908, when this photograph was taken by Fred Smith of the New York City Fire Department, colorful billboards advertising coming theater attractions had become commonplace on Times Square. The Times Tower itself was used for the first time in 1908 to drop the sparkling ball that to this day signifies the beginning of each New Year. Previously an apple had been dropped from the top of the tower. © *Collection of the New-York Historical Society, negative number 61055-410592*

Today it is impossible to miss the Times Tower — it has a 360-foot high electrified band circling the building to relay the day's news to passers-by. Enterprising ad man O. J. Gude first came up with the phrase "The Great White Way" in 1901 to describe the arrival of electricty-driven advertisements. It actually referred to Broadway around 34th Street but soon encompassed Times Square, too.

Left: Times Square in the rain in 1923, when *The Hunchback of Notre Dame* and *Rosita* were the films to see in the square's landmark cinemas. Virtual reality advertisements along "The Great White Way" included a man advertising cigarettes blowing real smoke rings, a girl blowing her nose on Kleenex, and soap bubbles billowing from a washing powder packet. An Irving Browning photograph.
© *Collection of the New-York Historical Society, negative number 58362*

Right: Times Square was once considered a somewhat tawdry area. Today the square has been cleaned up to the point where many people believe it resembles a giant theme park with only the neon advertisements reminding people of its history.

Times Square bustles almost as much during the day as at night and this photograph taken on New Year's Day 1930 shows pedestrians vying with vehicles along Broadway. The Times and Paramount buildings dominate the skyline, but nearby construction work shows the shape of things to come as other vacant lots fill up. *Hulton Getty Picture Collection*

The Marriott Marquis and its adjoining theater sit prominently on Times Square. This plush hotel, with a bank of glass elevators zooming up and down inside, has a revolving tower on its 48th floor allowing drinkers and diners to see the entire New York skyline as the tower slowly rotates over the course of one hour.

Left: Manhattan's skyline on June 17, 1948, as seen from the 70th floor of the RCA Building, the heart of the city-within-a-city Rockefeller Center. The view from this location — 49th and 50th Streets and Fifth and Sixth avenues — is dominated by the 1,250-foot Empire State Building and 699-foot 500 Fifth Avenue building at 42nd Street. The photograph was taken by New-York Historical Society's staff photographer, Charles T. Miller. © *Collection of the New-York Historical Society, negative number 30634*

Right: The Empire State Building, the world's tallest structure when it was completed in 1931, still dominates the skyline, but the 110-story twin towers of the former World Trade Center changed the landscape dramatically when they sprang up in 1977 on the tip of Lower Manhattan.

The Art Deco Radio City Hall was the brainchild of impresario Samuel "Roxy" Rothafel. The Roxy was his premiere cinema until the Rockefeller Center, originally 13 buildings spread over 11 acres of prime midtown land, took shape and Rothafel created what became the world's largest entertainment complex. *Hulton Getty Picture Collection*

Almost 700 major movies have made their debut at Radio City Hall and the dancing girls who originally appeared before each film were famous around the world as the Rockettes. In recent years, it has reverted back to live entertainment with major concerts, dance extravaganzas, and the annual Christmas special.

It took 75,000 men and ten years to build the Rockefeller Center, and by the time it was completed in 1934 America was in the midst of the Great Depression. Some 200 tenement buildings around 49th and 50th streets and Sixth and Fifth avenues were demolished to make way for financier John D. Rockefeller's dream "city within a city." This photograph, looking west from Fifth Avenue, was taken by Irving Browning about 1932. © *Collection of the New-York Historical Society, negative number 57849*

Today the Rockefeller Center consists of nineteen buildings, housing everything from corporate offices, restaurants, TV stations, and shops to the fabled Rainbow Room on the sixty-fifth floor of the RCA Building. The ice-skating rink — and home to New York's most lavish Christmas tree in December — is a major winter tourist attraction.

Work on St. Patrick's Cathedral on Fifth Avenue and 50th. Street actually began in 1858 but was put on hold during the Civil War. Finally completed in 1888, it is the largest Roman Catholic church in America. Ironically, it was considered to be practically out of town when work began, but by the time it was finally completed Manhattan had expanded uptown. © *Collection of the New-York Historical Society, negative number 32992*

Today Catholics from around the world make pilgrimages to St. Patrick's Cathedral and it represents the hopes and dreams of New York's Irish immigrants. James Renwick based his Gothic masterpiece, which seats 2,400 people, on a number of European churches — in particular Cologne Cathedral. Its twin spires are still a landmark on the New York skyline.

Left: By 1902, when this photograph of Fifth Avenue at 50th Street was taken, the area had become one of the ritziest neighborhoods in New York. Fancy shops and fabulous mansions lined the streets surrounding St. Patrick's Cathedral and the once muddy walkways had been replaced with pavements and proper roads. *Hulton Getty Picture Collection*

Right: Sitting alongside St. Patrick's is Saks Fifth Avenue, arguably New York's most fashionable department store. Saks Renaissance-inspired building complements the cathedral's Gothic architecture. Worshipers loaded down with the store's shopping bags often pop into St. Patrick's to light a candle.

The turn of the century was America's railway age, and when this photograph was taken in 1905 the current stretch of Park Avenue did not even exist. Grand Central Rail Depot's junction stretched a full ten blocks north from 42nd Street and provided a "resting ground" for trains like the "Twentieth Century Limited" and the "Empire Express." © *Collection of the New-York Historical Society, negative number 53661*

Park Avenue is New York's most dramatic boulevard. The dual roadway is separated by flowerbeds, and rents for both offices and apartments around 50th Street are the city's highest. The train tracks still exist, but they are now buried deep underground, where a labyrinth of tunnels take passengers out of Manhattan.

Left: Manhattan's social elite began moving uptown toward the end of the 19th century and the stretch of Fifth Avenue and 60th Street became one of the most sought-after residential districts. Grand mansions and beaux arts townhouses lined the boulevard, which offered fabulous views of Central Park just a stone's throw away.
Hulton Getty Picture Collection

Right: New York's premiere shopping district, Fifth Avenue is home to jeweler's Tiffany and Co.; despite the film title, it is impossible to have breakfast at Tiffany's because there has never been a restaurant. Other famous neighbors include luxury department store Bergdorf-Goodman, designer boutiques, and a host of other swanky stores.

The opening ribbon had just been cut when the 38-story Sherry-Netherland, then the world's tallest apartment hotel, caught fire on the night of April 20, 1927. Stunned New Yorkers converged on Fifth Avenue and the flames could be seen for miles around as the sky glowed red around the building. *Hulton Getty Picture Collection*

Hastily repaired, with a state-of-the-art fire alarm system added after the fire of 1927, the Sherry-Netherland is now one of New York's top hotels offering fabulous views of adjacent Central Park. Its slate-gray spire provides a skyline landmark for walkers lost in the middle of the park.

The Plaza, on Central Park South and 59th Street, dubbed itself New York's most luxurious hotel when it opened in 1907. With 800 rooms, heavily marbled lobby, spectacular Palm Court, restaurants, and wood-paneled Oak Room bar, it quickly became the social gathering place for Manhattan's elite. F. Scott Fitzgerald was a regular in the bar and wrote about it. *Hulton Getty Picture Collection*

After F. Scott Fitzgerald immortalized the Plaza in his "Roaring Twenties" tale *The Great Gatsby*, Kay Thompson followed with her children's books about Eloise, a little girl based on her goddaughter Liza Minnelli who lived in a Plaza Suite. It remains New York's top hotel and has been used in numerous films including *Home Alone II*.

Landscape architects Frederick Law Olmsted and Calvert Vaux spent twenty years clearing eighty acres of swampy New York to create the entirely artificial Central Park. They turned what was a wasteland of shanty towns and rubbish dumps into a rural jungle: New Yorkers loved it, as this 1894 May Day party reveals. © *Collection of the New-York Historical Society, negative number 51801*

A century on and Central Park has not lost its popular appeal. But anyone hoping for peace and quiet is in for a shock. The park is one of the most heavily used facilities in New York. Summer concerts begin in May and thousands converge to listen to pop and classical music concerts.

The winter of 1939 was a bitter one, but New Yorkers made the most of the freezing conditions by skating on Central Park's frozen lakes. Apart from the spire of the Carlyle Hotel at 76th and Madison Avenue, designed by architects Bien & Prince, standing majestically alone above the tree tops, it is still possible to believe one is in the middle of the countryside. © *Collection of the New-York Historical Society, negative number 6552*

Today the boating lake, and its adjoining restaurant, is one of the most popular spots in Central Park. In the heat of the summer young lovers can hire rowing boats and take picnics out on the water. But if they look up, they cannot miss the skyscraper apartment buildings that now dot the skyline.

Left: Ice skating has always been a favorite pastime of New Yorkers, and once summer officially ends after the first week of September, winter unofficially arrives and skating begins. When this picture was taken on September 23, 1913, there had been a sudden cold spell and Manhattanites dusted off their skates and dashed for the nearest frozen pond. © *Collection of the New-York Historical Society, negative number 48384*

Right: The notion of being in the countryside is long gone as the ritzy apartment blocks and state-of-the-art office buildings now overlook Central Park. However, for most New Yorkers the park is a major part of their lives. Joggers, roller bladers, and runners abound and families still enjoy picnics and boating on hot summer days.

Wooden shacks were common housing for poor New Yorkers in the 19th century and shanty towns lined the Hudson River. Little more than crude barns, livestock lived on the ground floor, while the family slept upstairs in the rafters. Fire was an ever-present danger and food was cooked outside well away from the shack. This is Riverside Drive between West 80th and 81st Streets. © Collection of the New-York Historical Society, negative number 46150

Central Park creator Frederick Law Olmsted began designing Riverside Park, along the Hudson River, in the 1880s, but it was finally finished by Clifford Lloyd in the 1930s. Mansions sprang up along Riverside Drive and the leafy adjoining streets are now home to superstars like Rolling Stone Mick Jagger.

The Cathedral of St. John the Divine was started in 1892 and will be the largest cathedral in the world when finished. Originally designed by Heins and LaFarge, the Gothic dimension was added by Ralph Adams Cram from 1911. This photograph, dated 1910, shows the Romanesque early design. *Hulton Getty Picture Collection*

This is a front view of the cathedral. Construction of the final phase started in 1979 and continues today. With the crossing tower in place, the front (west) towers completed, and the South Transept finished, it will be a truly awesome sight. © *Robert Holmes/Corbis*

City planners spotted the property potential of the Hudson River in the late 19th century and set about turning the Upper Westside and the Bronx into a booming residential area. Mansions, like the one pictured on Riverside Drive at 136th Street in 1908 for the Ottendorfers, began springing up. Frederick Law Olmsted designed the park and the road as a single entity. © *Collection of the New-York Historical Society, negative number 616*

Riverside Drive has maintained its earlier status as a residential haven. The old mansions have been pulled down but airy apartment blocks, mainly home to nearby Columbia University students, quickly replaced them.

The dramatic metal George Washington suspension bridge was not only a feat of incredible engineering, it took five years to complete and, for a brief while after its opening in 1931, was the world's largest suspension bridge at 3,500-feet long until that record was eclipsed by San Francisco's Golden Gate. Photograph by Erenest Scott. © *Collection of the New-York Historical Society, negative number 61772*

As the only New York city bridge to span the wide Hudson River, the George Washington can be seen for miles around, its gleaming steal suspension arches glinting in the sunshine. Thousands of motorists use it every day to reach Manhattan from Fort Lee in the neighboring state of New Jersey.

Cass Gilbert and O. H. Ammann's engineering master-piece, pictured shortly after its completion in 1931, provides an amazing view of the low buildings of upper Manhattan and the fast-moving Hudson River below. Early motorists caused havoc by slowing down to look at the scenery and catch a glimpse of the Little Red Lighthouse below. © *Collection of the New-York Historical Society, negative number 61741*

With traffic often at a crawl on the George Washington Bridge, day trippers consider the view from the top of the two-leveled roadway a sight-seeing must. The next Hudson bridge, the Tappan Zee 25 miles upstate in Tarrytown, can be seen on a clear day along with the Manhattan skyline.

Left: Billionaire James Lenox's fortune helped to build New York Public Library and, in return for his legacy, the city named Lenox Avenue in his honor. This wide boulevard, pictured here in 1930, was lined with smart apartment blocks where wealthy citizens made their homes and showed off their new cars. *Hulton Getty Picture Collection*

Right: Harlem around Lenox Avenue and 133rd Street has seen better days. Many New Yorkers refuse to go further than 125th Street but in the final years of the 20th century the area went through another metamorphosis. New businesses and chain stores are moving in and the district is booming once again.

Baseball is America's national pastime and on May 31, 1886, when this photograph was taken, the New York Giants reigned supreme. The Polo Ground, at Fifth Avenue and 110th Street, was considered hallowed ground. The stadium had low seating, unlike today's grand arenas, but already the game was attracting big crowds and advertising. © *Collection of the New-York Historical Society, negative number 32485*

Sports fans still complain about the Giants moving out of New York to San Francisco in 1957. Before then both the Giants and the Yankees had moved to a new Polo Ground on 155th Street at the turn of the century and today Fifth Avenue at 110th Street is a low-rent residential district.

INDEX